11/11/19

To my dear friend, fellow traveller, nature lover, gardener, & appreciator of beauty & wonder...

A GATELESS GARDEN

I look forward to more explorations with you & cultivation of gateless gardens

♡

Jace

A GATELESS GARDEN

Quotes by
MAINE WOMEN WRITERS

Editor Liza Bakewell

Photographer Kerry Michaels

Assistant Editor Meygan Lackey

 A Maine Women Write Book

Excerpt from WITHOUT A MAP by Meredith Hall, copyright © 2007 by Meredith Hall. Reprinted by permission of Beacon Press, Boston. All rights reserved.

Excerpt from LOVING AND LEAVING THE GOOD LIFE by Helen Nearing, copyright © 1992 by Helen Nearing. Used by permission of Chelsea Green Publishing, White River Junction, Vermont. All rights reserved.

Excerpt from THE SENSE OF WONDER by Rachel Carson, copyright © 1956 by Rachel Carson. Reprinted by permission of Frances Collin, Trustee.

Excerpt from EUPHORIA by Lily King, copyright © 2014 by Lily King. Grove/Atlantic, Inc. All rights reserved.

Excerpt from WHEN WE WERE THE KENNEDYS by Monica Wood, copyright © 2012 by Monica Wood. Used by permission of Houghton Mifflin Harcourt. All rights reserved.

Excerpt from MY GARDEN OF MEMORY: AN AUTOBIOGRAPHY by Kate Douglas Wiggin, copyright ©1923 by Kate Douglas Wiggin. Used by permission of Houghton Mifflin Harcourt. All rights reserved.

Excerpt from GLASS MOUNTAIN by Cynthia Voigt, copyright © 1991 by Cynthia Voigt. Used by permission of Houghton Mifflin Harcourt. All rights reserved.

Excerpt from THE ISLANDERS by Elizabeth Foster, copyright © 1946 by Elizabeth Foster. Used by permission of Houghton Mifflin Harcourt. All rights reserved.

Excerpt from WE TOOK TO THE WOODS by Louise Dickinson Rich, copyright © 1942 by Louise Dickinson Rich. Used by permission of HarperCollins Publishers LLC. All rights reserved.

Excerpt from THIS LIFE IS IN YOUR HANDS by Melissa Coleman, copyright © 2011 by Melissa Coleman. Used by permission of HarperCollins Publishers LLC. All rights reserved.

Excerpt from ORPHAN TRAIN by Christina Baker Kline, copyright © 2013 by Christina Baker Kline. Used by permission of HarperCollins Publishers LLC. All rights reserved.

Excerpt from PEGGY SUE GOT MURDERED by Tess Gerritson, copyright © 1994 by Tess Gerritson. Used by permission of HarperCollins Publishers LLC. All rights reserved.

Excerpt from I SLEEP AROUND by Nadya Bernard copyright © 1979 by Nadya Bernard. Reprinted with the permission of Literati Press. All rights reserved.

Excerpt from "Lethe" from COLLECTED POEMS by Edna St. Vincent Millay, copyright © 1928, 1955 by Edna St. Vincent Millay and Norma Millay Ellis. Reprinted with the permission of The Permissions Company, Inc., on behalf of Holly Peppe, Literaray Executor, The Millay Society, www.miillay.org. All rights reserved.

Excerpt from THE GIFT FROM THE SEA by Anne Morrow Lindbergh, copyright © 1955, 1975, copyright renewed 1983 by Anne Morrow Lindbergh. Used by permission of Pantheon Books, an imprint of the Knopf Doubleday Publishing Group, a division of Random House LLC. All rights reserved.

Excerpt from WHITE DOG FELL FROM THE SKY by Eleanor Morse, copyright © 2013 by Eleanor Morse. Used by permission of Viking Penguin, a division of Penguin Group (USA) LLC. All rights reserved.

Excerpt from SIGHT AND SENSIBILITY: THE ECOPSYCHOLOGY OF PERCEPTION by Laura Sewall, copyright © 1999 by Laura Sewall. Used by permission of Jeremy P. Tarcher, an imprint of Penguin Group (USA) LLC. All rights reserved.

Excerpt from RED RUBY HEART IN A COLD BLUE SEA by Morgan Callan Rogers, copyright © 2012 by Morgan Callan Rogers. Used by permission of Viking Penguin, a division of Penguin Group (USA) LLC. All rights reserved.

Excerpt from POSTCARDS by E. Annie Proulx, copyright © 1992 by E. Annie Proulx. Reprinted with permission of Scribner Publishing Group, a division of Simon & Schuster, Inc. All rights reserved.

Excerpt from OUR WAY DOWN EAST by Elinor Graham, copyright © 1943, 1971 by Elinor Graham. Reprinted with permission of Scribner Publishing Group, a division of Simon & Schuster, Inc. All rights reserved.

Excerpt from MARY PETERS by Mary Ellen Chase, copyright © 1934 by Mary Ellen Chase. Reprinted with permission of Scribner Publishing Group, a division of Simon & Schuster, Inc. All rights reserved.

Excerpt from SWEET RELIEF OF MISSING CHILDREN by Sarah Braunstein, copyright © 2011 by Sarah Braunstein. Used by permission of W. W. Norton & Company. All rights reserved.

Excerpt from AS WE ARE NOW by May Sarton, copyright © 1973 by May Sarton. Used by permission of W. W. Norton & Company. All rights reserved.

Excerpt from LATE PSALM by Betsy Sholl, copyright © 2004 by the Board of Regents of the University of Wisconsin System. Reprinted by permission of the University of Wisconsin Press. All rights reserved.

Excerpt from THE SOUND OF A WILD SNAIL EATING by Elizabeth Tova Bailey, copyright © 2010 Elizabeth Tova Bailey. Used by permission of Workman Publishing. All rights reserved.

Excerpt from SETTLED IN THE WILD: NOTES FROM THE EDGE OF TOWN by Susan Hand Shetterly, copyright © 2010 by Susan Hand Shetterly. Used by permission of Workman Publishing. All rights reserved.

Excerpt from A BRIEF LUNACY by Cynthia Thayer, copyright © 2005 by Cynthia Thayer. Used by permission of Workman Publishing. All rights reserved.

Excerpt from THE GARDEN PRIMER by Barbara Damrosch, copyright © 2008 by Barbara Damrosch. Used by permission of Workman Publishing. All rights reserved.

Additional permissions were received directly from authors Siri Beckman, Carolyn Chute, Susan Conley, Sara Corbett, Carol Dana, Annie Finch, Carolyn Gage, Alan Hall for Martha Hall, Tabitha King, Carol Leonard, Cathie Pelletier, Mary Plouffe, Lee Sharkey, Debra Spark, Pam Cunningham for ssipsis, Linda Tatelbaum, and Barbara Walsh; as well as from the following publishers: About Time Press, Bad Beaver Publishing, Bowman Books, Gary Lawless, Islandport Press, Kensington Press, Monmouth Press, Robin Hood Press, Roman and Littlefield, Tilbury House, and Vanguard.

Printing by Thomson-Shore, Dexter, MI

Book design by Cheryl Carrington
Bakewell, Liza
Michaels, Kerry
A gateless garden: Quotes by Maine women writers / — 1st ed.
ISBN: 978-0-9707615-1-4

Maine Women Write

www.mainewomenwrite.org

1 2 3 4 5 6 7 8 9 0

CONTENTS

INTRODUCTION

I hope every woman who can write will not be silent.
Harriet Beecher Stowe, 1850, Brunswick, Maine

Maine has been home to great women authors—erudite, wise, and passionate—whose writing has changed the world. Women in Maine, armed with pen and paper, have influenced the outcome of the Civil War, mobilized women's political and domestic rights, and powered the creation of the U.S. Environmental Protection Agency. They have upset the status quo again and again. Many of them—not only the well known—have made this world a better place. As director of Maine Women Write, an organization that promotes the works of Maine women writers, I thought right now must be a perfect time to collectively celebrate our half of Maine's literary history.

What makes a Maine woman writer? To answer that question, I looked to the Maine Women Writers Collection (MWWC) at the University of New England and found these criteria for inclusion in its extensive collections: At some point in her life, the author lived and wrote in Maine, and Maine influenced her writing. Most of the women writers gathered here have lived in Maine for many years—some their entire lives—and have produced in Maine the works quoted in this book. Others who are quoted, passed through. Harriet Beecher Stowe was born and died in Connecticut, but she wrote *Uncle Tom's Cabin* in Brunswick, Maine, where she lived for two years. The story line, which came to her during a service held at the First Parish Church, was sharpened by discussions with local, abolitionist friends. Louise Bogan was born in Maine and lived here off and on as a young child before she moved away, but her Maine childhood, tumultuous as it was, seeded her poetry and feminism of later years. Anne Morrow Lindbergh spent long summers in Maine with her husband and family; her references to sea and land, no matter the book, are deeply informed by her love of Penobscot Bay and her observations of island life. Edna St. Vincent Millay left her home in Camden at the age of twenty-one to attend Vassar College. She did not return to live year-round, yet Millay considered Maine her home, visiting her mother in Camden frequently as well as spending summers on Ragged Island in Casco Bay. Rachel Carson was born in Pennsylvania and worked in Washington, D.C., but it was when she first came to Maine on a visit as an adult that she truly felt at home; here was a place where she could write peacefully, while observing the intricacies of the natural world. A common theme emerges, not only among these notable authors, but among all others found here: for over two hundred years Maine has inspired women to write.

Collecting quotes from full-length works might have brought with it some irreconcilable challenges—orphaned stanzas, homeless lines—if it had not been for the exquisite writing Maine women have penned; each quote stands tall on its own. My assistant, Meygan Lackey, and I felt privileged to spend two years reading their prose and poetry. But that is not the whole quote-collecting story. There was another privilege in store. Early on in the project, Maine writer and photographer, Kerry Michaels, suggested that a synergy might evolve from matching the quotes with photographs of Maine—its gardens, lakes, mountains, fields, and ocean. Taken by the idea, we set to pairing the two media. The result was alchemy. The interplay of words and photos enlivened each and, above all, accentuated just how much Maine women writers have energized the essence of place, strengthened women's lives, and illuminated the human condition.

Liza Bakewell, Freeport, Maine

For

Avery and Jennie

Brett, Ethan, and Maya

and our Moms

ACKNOWLEDGMENTS

Many thanks to the Maine women writers represented here who generously gave us permission to use their words and to all the publishing houses that granted us permission to use quotes from their published works. We are grateful, as well, to Cathleen Miller, Curator, and Catherine Fischer, Assistant, at the Maine Women Writers Collection, University of New England, for their generous support while we perused the archives; to Anne B. Zill, Director, University of New England Art Gallery, for exhibiting the quotes and photographs at the gallery; and to the Freeport Community Library for having a strong collection of works by Maine women writers. Special thanks to Avery Bakewell, Jennie Bakewell, Polly Oakleaf Bakewell, Chris Beach, Kathy Biberstein, Mary Ann Biberstein, Chris Bowe, Lisa Bowe, Kevin Callahan, Cheryl Carrington, Mark Chimsky, Anne Depue, Diane Dreher, Judy Maloney, Sybil Masquelier, Brian Mattlin, Janet McTeer, Gina Michaels, Glenna Michaels, Polly Nichols, Jim Nickelson, Nicole Olivier, Deborah Pfeffer, Brett Pierce, Ethan Pierce, Maya Pierce, Mary Plouffe, Sue Reed, Jessica Skwire Routhier, Megan Thorn, David Treadwell, Scott Vile, and Fiona Wilson.

A GATELESS GARDEN

The world is mine: blue hill, still silver lake,
Broad field, bright flower, and the long white road
A gateless garden, and an open path;
My feet to follow, and my heart to hold.

Edna St. Vincent Millay, 1917

Looking down,
I saw the earth beneath me like a rose
petaled with mountains,
fragrant with deep peace.

Elizabeth Coatsworth, 1924

There was no sound but that of a cricket; no ripple on the great smooth lake; nothing had moved recently enough to leave a circle on its surface within half a mile; yet, slowly, not five rods from me, out of the heart of the quiet water, rose the green head and neck of a loon.

Fannie Hardy Eckstorm, 1901

The land was a passion, magical in its influence upon human life. It produced people; nothing else at all, except trees and flowers and vegetable harvests. Life ran back and forth, land into people and people back into land, until both were the same.

Lura Beam, 1957

Have you ever seen a deer's horns in the velvet? or a cow moose with two young trotting down an open road? or come upon an ancient graveyard in neglect where foxes make their dens inside each grave?

Elinor Graham, 1943

Those who dwell, as scientists or laymen, among the beauties and mysteries of the earth are never alone or weary of life.

Rachel Carson, 1956

I need beauty, laughter, love and gladness,
    Music coming softly from afar
Courage for the night, and through the darkness,
    I need to see the glimmer of a star.

Ina Ladd Brown, 1946

When the winters finally leave, they leave of their own accord, and behind them lie the cabin fever dreams, those sentiments which have lain dormant as autumn seeds, waiting for the right temperature, the right caress of sunlight, the proper texture of soil to sprout. And after five months of snow, what man is so hardened that he does not melt at the sight of buds on the wild cherry? What deer does not lift its ears to the first music of the old river running free again, shed of its blanket of ice? What woman does not scan the damp earth in the field near her house so closely that her eye can finally trace the ghostly outlines of cucumber beds, sweet peas, and all the fiery carrots she will grow there in a garden when the land is dry enough?

Cathie Pelletier, 1989

When she saw the red buds against the delicate blue and white, she knew there were some things that would always fire her spirit. Red buds, and the first roseate flush along the apple boughs, the first blue birds to light on raspberry canes in the field— she always forgot how blue they were; the early morning crying of the gulls circling and calling over the harbor after their winter silence; the new traps outside the fish houses, and the repainted buoys hung in the sun like beads to be strung by a giant, red and yellow, blue and white, black and orange.

Elisabeth Ogilvie, 1947

From the top of the hill the terrace had the color and substance of the restless blue ocean off the coast of Maine—an inland sea of cobalt and ultramarine and sapphire, tipped with a froth of pure white flowers. All you could see were lupines—no raspberries or pigweed or dandelions—just an acre of blue flowers, tossing in the wind.

Elizabeth Foster, 1946

She learned, from blossom in the wild,
From bird upon the wing,
From silence and the midnight stars,
Truth dwells in everything.

Elizabeth Oakes Smith, 1845

I rejoice as if I were newborn, seeing with wide-open eyes, as only the old can (for the newborn infant cannot see) the marvels of the world.

May Sarton, 1973

For within my heart's eye I see

    The tiny bud struggling to give bloom to beauty

    And the tiny egg waiting to give wing to wind

I yearn for truth and purity of earth life

    And when I stumble over them

    I become shy at their love

My drum ceases to call their spirit, they are here and now

Mumble my thanks and whisper my acknowledgement

    To creation which still fulfills its purpose

Sometimes I cry when within the grey sidewalk concrete

    I see a tiny blade of grass

I greet the one who has struggled to be

ssipsis, 2007

If I had influence with the good fairy who is supposed to preside over the christening of all children I should ask that her gift to each child in the world be a sense of wonder so indestructible that it would last throughout life, as an unfailing antidote against the boredom and disenchantments of later years, the sterile preoccupation with things that are artificial, the alienation from the sources of our strength.

Rachel Carson, 1956

It is hard
to understand, to see that all my old dreams
have contracted just
into this, an August afternoon, the glint
of pale blue chicory in the ditch, touch-me-not
hanging orange above it, asters
reaching across the tangle of tired leaves—
dry, darkened, thickly grown, turning brittle—
like drifts of light beside the road, stitches
on a rough, unrolling cloth, as white and open
as the stars they are.

Kate Barnes, 2004

Once you have befriended even one herb, you will be presented with an enduring relationship that will be a constant source of wisdom and joy.

Deb Soule, 1995

Take a different direction,
wind.
Restore our world again
Let us walk in balance
Let us dance again
Let us Begin again
Let us be kind again
Let us be again
Put our prayers to the four winds,
Our hopes to the sky,
Our feet to the earth, again.

Carol Dana (Red Hawk/pipikwass), 2011

WHY SHE WRITES

Women were supposed to follow. But what if men didn't lead? Women were supposed to wait. But what if they waited and waited and nothing happened?

Virginia Chase, 1971

An absolute, archaic grief possessed this countrywoman; she seemed like a renewal of some historic soul, with her sorrows and the remoteness of a daily life busied with rustic simplicities and the scents of primeval herbs.

Sarah Orne Jewett, 1896

I must recall my childhood and its externalities; I must paint the portrait of the little child, that you may better comprehend the woman; and show you the bud in which so many embryo leaves lay folded and almost invisible, that you may recognise the flower when it blooms into the fulness of glowing, panting, luxuriant life.

Margaret J. M. Sweat, 1859

I write what I cannot say.

I paint in colors fearsome and strange.

I make marks with meaning only in their making.

I make books so I won't die.

Help me read them to you.

Martha Hall, 2001

O God, why were women born with ambition! I wish I could sit and tat, instead of wanting to go and write the poem, or lie and kiss the ground.

Louise Bogan, 1924

I write as often as not out of a self-induced, incantatory dream state, chanting and acting out my poems as I compose.

Annie Finch, 2005

Survival often depends on a specific focus: a relationship, a belief, or a hope balanced on the edge of possibility. Or something more ephemeral: the way the sun passes through the hard, seemingly impenetrable glass of a window and warms the blanket, or how the wind, invisible but for its wake, is so loud one can hear it through the insulated walls of a house.

Elisabeth Tova Bailey, 2010

While you're running around in your brain, all the time the sun only wishes to wake you to its beauty.

Eleanor Morse, 2013

She lived by snatches, by fits and starts, by spurts of desperate effort, and had for years; sometimes it seemed she could not stand the strain of it; but lately it was different; she could manage.

Gladys Hasty Carroll, 1933

This was the start of a secret game, a game she had played all her life, especially when she was troubled. You would open a book just anywhere, run your finger down a page, stop suddenly, and tell yourself that that verse or line had something in it pertaining to you. It wasn't a game, really, for you didn't take a game seriously; and of course she didn't take this seriously, though it was surprising how many times it had worked out.

Virginia Chase, 1953

Some fair and beautiful women too, whose minds are too capacious, to be bound within the narrow, and confined limits that the sex have been obliged to walk by; have thrown off the fetters of prejudice, and advanced within the circle of the illuminated; these are the persons, whose births and fortunes are inferior to none.

Madame Sally Wood, 1800

I like women who don't like the way things are.

Carolyn Gage, 1999

The spectre of independent women brings fear to the hearts of those who would maintain their power and privilege.

Perdita Huston, 1992

And what if delight and pleasure, instead of torture and sacrifice, were considered sacred? What if nobody needed to be born again, because the first time was considered sacred enough? What if . . . a woman's sexuality was considered a divine gift instead of a pornographic resource?

Carolyn Gage, 2008

She decided to be a poet, imagining poets to be terribly misunderstood but true to themselves.

Lee Sharkey, 1986

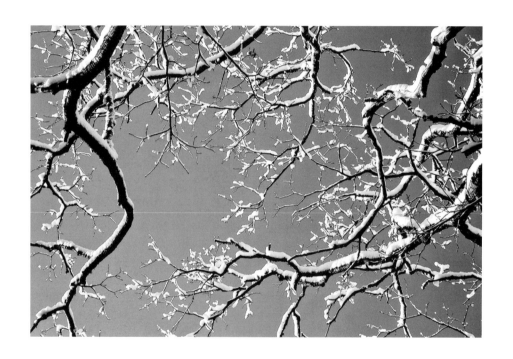

Of course, in a novel, people's hearts break, and they die, and that is the end of it; and in a story this is very convenient. But in real life we do not die when all that makes life bright dies to us.

Harriet Beecher Stowe, 1852

Experience has taught me a little; not very much, and only at the expense of profound and exhausting effort.

Kate Douglas Wiggin, 1923

This is what I can't decide:—whether I don't have any spare time at all, or whether most of my time is spare time.

Louise Dickinson Rich, 1942

When I cannot write a poem, I bake biscuits and feel just as pleased.

Anne Morrow Lindbergh, 1955

Simple, busy, contented child of long ago, peering at me out of the haze of the past, I wonder how much of her survives in me to-day!

Kate Douglas Wiggin, 1923

My acceptance and love of this life make passivity impossible. The more I love it the more I care about its fate, our fate, want to protect the suffering seas, the weeds, the air, the spawn, and each neglected old woman.

Alix Kates Shulman, 1995

Who am I to think that I will figure it all out by writing in my notebook?

Cynthia Thayer, 2005

LOVE AND LONGING

You are a question, small and dense,
and I am an answer, long diffuse
and dark, but I want to be sky
for you so, like the stars, I lie,

holding my far lights wide and flat
in pictures for your eyes to take,
spaced easily, so you can catch
the patterns in your sleepy net.

Annie Finch, 1997

Gone is the fever,
But not into the river;
Melted the frozen pride,
But the tranquil tide
Runs never the warmer for this,
Never the colder.

Immerse the dream.
Drench the kiss.
Dip the song in the stream.

Edna St. Vincent Millay, 1928

"When I looked at you," he said, "singing that simple hymn that first day, I felt as I do when I look at the evening star leaning out of the clear sunset lustre: there is something in your face as pure, as remote, as shining. It will always be there," he said, "though you should live a hundred years." He little knew. He little knew!

Harriet Prescott Spofford, 1900

We walked miles, over the rock-strewn pastures, to favorite spots along the shore for picnics. We were young, and vigorous, and productive, and lighthearted.

Miriam Colwell, 1950s

What a day! Not sunny but wickedly bright, the sky white as snow and silver at the horizon. . . . The birds hovered but did not land. . . . [She] looked for a long time at that tree. Every other day she'd seen it as any-old-tree, but today it struck her as alive, beautiful, and she wished it were summer and she could climb it. She knew herself, accepted who she was, but sometimes it was true, she envied tomboys in bandannas who scrambled up trees, girls with scraped knees who didn't apply ointment or Band-Aids. This was the tree she'd climb, if she were that girl.

Sarah Braunstein, 2011

Will we ever stop longing to feel
   feathers spread out from our arms, a tail
      at our waists, little twiggy feet—and blue,
can we please be blue?

Betsy Sholl, 2004

He turned as she entered, and looked at the girl he had loved so long—she was still a girl to [him]; he saw the sweet face, the pansy-trimmed bonnet, the black mantilla over a shimmering lavender silk dress; he saw the faint excitement in the myrtle-blue eyes; he never saw the little wrinkles or the gray hairs.

Margaret Deland, 1898

Passion. The conduit through which every unseen thing will rush.

Carolyn Chute, 1994

We fell into . . . bed like one body, coiled around each other like eels. He was part of me before I knew it. His hands touched me in ways that didn't hurt, as if he knew where all my scars were. My legs wrapped him tight and we dove deep, past the seaweed, past the bottom of the ocean.

Morgan Callan Rogers, 2012

He seemed to know no difference between men's and women's places and was neither awkward nor ashamed to be heard speaking of such things as the colors in the sky.

Gladys Hasty Carroll, 1933

Rain that falls in the long surprise that is us together
bundled on hard sand, listening to stone water.

Thick night pools around our bones and faces
until we can barely reach each other's outlines tenderly.

We are an invention of each heart climbing out of itself.
The ghost of a dark barn in the dunes seals what is between us.

Susan Conley, 2002

I try not to return to these moments very often, for I end up lacerating my young self for not simply kissing the girl. I thought we had time. Despite everything, I believed somehow there was time. Love's first mistake. Perhaps love's only mistake. Time for you and time for me. . . . And what would it have mattered in the end? What would it have altered to have kissed her then, that night? Everything. Nothing. Impossible to know.

Lily King, 2014

Secret love is fragile, but true love should be able to withstand exposure.

Alix Kates Shulman, 1995

Maybe I'll drive you crazy and you'll drive me crazy.
Maybe we'll bounce around on the edge of madness,
trying to weave our lives together. Is it worth it?

He smiled. She smiled.

And they both knew, without saying a word, that he would always do what it took to keep her.

And she would stay.

Tess Gerritsen, 1994

Love is not a word. Love is a tough gnarl, a solid burl. There is no edge to get under, no way to lift it out and examine it, no evidence for and against it, no etiology nor teleology, no —ology at all. Love Is.

Linda Tatelbaum, 2009

In between their work and worry, the widows often stared at the bay and sobbed. They spoke to the water as if it would somehow talk back to them, render the secrets of where their husbands' bodies lay hidden.

Barbara Walsh, 2012

The coffee. Its blackness in the familiar blue cups. He stirred in the sugar, Her spoon clinked.

Then all at once the awkwardness was gone. Stories of things he had seen began to pour out, the words firing from between his loosened and gapped teeth. . . . He, who had talked little, talked much, swelled to a glowing huckster selling stories of his life.

Annie Proulx, 1992

For a woman, marriage is a natural step after love, so she quite wisely hesitates at love.

Cynthia Voigt, 1991

She thought if they were ever together, their lives would begin to weave just like this, one small hurt, a backing down and recovery, another and another until a tapestry was woven, as complicated as any other. The euphoria of newness would last a month, two months, a year, and then they'd be caught in something of their making and beyond their making.

Eleanor Morse, 2013

Contrast . . . appears as the sharp, shiny edge of black rock against a bright blue sky. It is the edge between dark and light, between round red berries and brilliant green leaves. . . . It is a thin line of branch across a full moon, a star against the night sky. It is the edge of water on shore . . . and the difference between faith and doubt.

Laura Sewall, 1999

Nothing blooms when watched. Avert your gaze, and wait, and hope.

Linda Tatelbaum, 2004

It is not always in gold days, but in gray ones, that the soul grows and the purpose of life unfolds.

Kate Douglas Wiggin, 1923

We speak volumes, you and I, in our silence. . . . I sit a mile away, across a space littered with wounds I can only imagine. "But I can imagine," my silence says, and I am still here. . . . I know the silence that follows just the right words, the ones that fall unbidden from my lips or yours, surprising us both with their astonishingly obvious truth.

Mary E. Plouffe, 2011

Most people were wrong about life, she thought. It was not a struggle against temptation as she had been taught in church. Nor was it a search for truth as the philosophers said, or even for happiness, much as humanity craved happiness. It was rather a kind of waiting—a waiting upon the graciousness and bounty of the things which had been, in order that the things to come might find one free and unafraid.

Mary Ellen Chase, 1934

I ain't seen him for some years; he's forgot our youthful feelin's, I expect, but a woman's heart is different; them feelin's comes back when you think you've done with 'em, as sure as spring comes with the year.

Sarah Orne Jewett, 1896

What young people didn't know, she thought, lying down beside this man, his hand on her shoulder, her arm; oh, what young people did not know. They did not know that lumpy, aged, and wrinkled bodies were as needy as their own young, firm ones, that love was not to be tossed away carelessly, as if it were a tart on a platter with others that got passed around again. No, if love was available, one chose it, or didn't choose it. And if her platter had been full with the goodness of Henry and she had found it burdensome, had flicked it off crumbs at a time, it was because she had not known what one should know: that day after day was unconsciously squandered.

Elizabeth Strout, 2008

There are in this world blessed souls, whose sorrows all spring up into joys for others; whose earthly hopes, laid in the grave with many tears, are the seed from which spring healing flowers and balm for the desolate and distressed. Among such was the delicate woman who sits there by the lamp, dropping slow tears.

Harriet Beecher Stowe, 1852

"You know," he says, no effort to keep the edge out of his voice, "if I knew what to do, I wouldn't have come here."

"Well," she says mildly, "really you have to figure out what you most want."

"What I want" he says, "is to do the least harm, and I want you to tell me of what that might consist."

"Oh," she says, again evenly, apparently practiced in the art of disappointing. "I can't do that."

Debra Spark, 2011

We turned and walked down the path, toward the shining waters of the lake, in a reflective and pensive mood, leaving behind us the poignant stories told by the gravestones in the little cemetery.

Mary R. Calvert, 1986

I can't help thinking

It's possible there is no death at all,
just a thin veil between one life and another,
lifting sometimes in a wail, or wind, an eddy

of leaves wrapping itself around the legs
of a grieving mother, or telling a child
it's all right, all right now, to let go.

Betsy Sholl, 2004

[She] follows her gaze to the Rorschach shapes of the apple trees, barely visible in the light from the house. "I can honestly say that I never regretted marrying him. But you know the rest, so I will tell you this. I did love him. But I did not love him like I loved Dutchy: beyond reason. Maybe you only get one of those in a lifetime, I don't know. But it was all right. It was enough."

Christina Baker Kline, 2013

It was one of those nights when she felt an onrush of loneliness. . . . The bed looked big and cold, the towering headboard was too imposing for a woman sleeping alone. She turned back the covers so that they would look more hospitable, and began to undress. After the itching nervousness she'd felt downstairs, her skin received the cool air gratefully. She stood naked for a moment, rejoicing in her freedom from clothes as simply as an animal enjoys freedom from its harness.

Elisabeth Ogilvie, 1947

I've come to think that's what heaven is—a place in the memory of others where our best selves live on.

Christina Baker Kline, 2013

Perhaps there is only one sin—separateness—with the blessedness of love making all whole. I feel that life is such a unity that love which once happened still exists. It is there on the record. Love once felt has its place.

Helen Nearing, 1992

HOME

Through the windy night something
      is coming up the path
      towards the house.
I have always hated to wait for things.
      I think I will go
      to meet whatever it is.

              Elizabeth Coatsworth, 1976

There is something about a farmhouse that no other dwelling possesses—an individuality, an aura of permanence and peace.

Ina Ladd Brown, 1953

His old farmhouse stands firm, well maintained and owned by another family now, but the open fields, barns, woods, and ponds look the same. There is an orchard where cattle once grazed, the big vegetable garden lies fallow, and there is no wartime egg production—but there *could* be.

Martha White, 2013

All ordinary people like us, everywhere, are trying to find the same things. . . .
They all want to be left alone to conduct their own private search for a personal
peace, a reasonable security, a little love, a chance to attain happiness through
achievement. It isn't much to want; but I never came anywhere near to getting
most of those things until we took to the woods.

Louise Dickinson Rich, 1942

The winter after my daughter was born, I would set her in her carrier, put it on my back, and take her in the afternoons, before dusk, into the woods. I believed that even if she fell asleep, which she always did, the trees, the tracks of wild animals in the snow, the dead leaves rattling on the branches, the hoot of an owl, a grouse feeding on birch catkins—everything—would pass into her life and make it good.

Susan Hand Shetterly, 2010

I remember thinking, with the endless blue sky above, the light, the color and smell of apples and earth and trees and fall, the mountains and valley in the distance, that I was finally at peace. My life had come back to a kind of order. I knew who I was, where I was meant to be. It was here in this place, with my small, brave family, that I found some kind of Eden.

Caitlin Shetterly, 2011

At the bridge, I remembered a friend saying that crossing to our island on a summer day was like traveling up the stem of a marvelous flower.

Siri Beckman, 1992

I wish, dear love, we had a world,
    A world that's all our own,
Not large enough for wealth and power,
    But just for us alone;
A fairy island far away
    In some bright southern sea,
Where skies should shine and earth should smile
    Only for you and me, dear love,
      Only for you and me!

Elizabeth Akers Allen, 1856

I am astounded. Another squeeze comes. I look at the clock. Twenty minutes apart. I get up quietly and walk around to see if the contractions stop. I pace around our bedroom loft. I look out the window to the trees, shadowy in the soft moonlight. I am tingling with anticipation.

Carol Leonard, 2008

You are filled with a new intention. Something stretches beyond you, drawing you along, and as you move forward in a dark place you can barely make out shapes and your face feels invisible. No one sees you anymore. You don't think it, but you have the odd feeling: Maybe this will lead me home.

Susan Minot, 2014

The human body absorbs minerals from the soil in the area we grow up. . . .
These minerals bind with our teeth and bones, and bind us to the earth itself.

Meredith Hall, 2007

I may not be able to anticipate everything you want to know, but I will explain how pruning can make your plants bushier, more compact, or more fruitful. I will tell you that mulch is a layer of material, such as shredded bark, that you lay down on the ground chiefly to keep weeds from growing and to keep the soil moist. And I will try to come to your aid when you're standing there alone in the garden, holding a plant that looks like an amorphous tangle, and you have no idea what to do with it. If I could go out there with you, I would tell you what my nurseryman friends . . . used to tell their fledgling workers: "Plant it with the green side up." Everyone has to start somewhere.

Barbara Damrosch, 2008

Soon will snow be flying, soon will tempests roar,
Soon the freezing north will lash us bitter as
      before;
I heard the waters whisper, I heard the winds
      complain,
But sweet, reluctant Summer I knew would come
      again.

Celia Thaxter, 1878

Everywhere I could hear, smell and feel the snow melting. I loved these days of wet metamorphosis when all the winter colors were suddenly liquid.

Siri Beckman, 1992

But I like winter, that most compelling season, when the air crackles audibly with cold; when the stars plead to be touched, to be plucked for a lucent torch to light a path, they hang so closely down; when Northern lights waver a lambent curtain from out the pole; when the dull and dreary earth and trees adorn themselves from top to toe, in purest white. . . . Winter, my time of muted tranquility, my time of impenetrable impregnability in my cozy cocoon; winter, my time of relief, at last, from authoritarian intrusions on my id, when I am holed up alone, within my fortress of surrounding snow.

Nadya Bernard, 1979

What she sees for the future takes some consideration. Oh, she supposes she will meet more people and they will fit into her life in quiet order. They step from the edges of dream and say hello. We will talk of our lives. We will enjoy the composition of a simple glass of Cabernet placed on a white windowsill, sun and ivy and narrow border of clean ecru lace. For she has already learned to love old things. They are harmonious with [her] soul.

Carolyn Chute, 1994

She couldn't formulate, much less say out loud, that she was beginning to see this daily routine as the blueprint of family life, of her life—that there would be nothing more than these fields, these swollen knuckles, this long day. She had no word for 'uninspired,' or the belief that her mind was meant for something different. . . . Because she had no words for these emotions, she couldn't yet process the converse: that this life was a choice for many in the northern Maine community, that it had merit and taught, among other things, the value of work and people and money. She had no idea that as an adult, she might be proud and grateful for the potato-picking experience, this ride home with her stepfather.

Shonna Milliken Humphrey, 2011

The men weren't romantic, or daring, or glamorous. But they were something much better. They were good neighbors.

Louise Dickinson Rich, 1942

My neighbor toils with wise and patient hand,
Scarce pausing in his work for sun or shower,
Evolving gradually from mould and sand
The germ, the leaf, the perfect bud and flower.

Elizabeth Akers Allen, 1886

One day, [she] arrived at my cabin with a beaming smile and said something
I'm quite certain that nobody else, as long as I live, will ever say to me again. "I had
so much fun making a cake for you earlier today," she said. This didn't mean she'd
pulled out a box of Duncan Hines and her electric mixer, but rather that she'd gotten
up at 5 a.m. to build the fire to heat the antique oven for my cake, and then she'd
stood in her wild little kitchen as the sun came up, intently sifting flour, shaving
delicate vanilla beans, and grinding nutmeg to get the flavor just so. That cake was,
in every sense of the word, divine.

Sara Corbett, 2009

In the muggy night, her dreams flowered, gorgeous and exotic. She was in the kitchen, cooking. Stirring a big pot fragrant with filé gumbo. She realized she was naked and laughed, happy as a child in her bath. In fact, she was a child in her bath, the pot transformed into the tin-cup measures her mother had given her for tub toys.

Tabitha King, 1988

Some say hands hold the map of our lives; that the lines of the palm correspond with the heart, head, and soul to create a story unique to each of us. Understanding the lines is an attempt to understand why things happen as they do. Also a quick way to figure out who might make a good neighbor.

Melissa Coleman, 2011

At the appointed hour, my husband and I gather around the stove to take the pie out of the oven. The crust is lightly browned, looking neither tough nor chewy. The thick purple berry juice bubbles around the edges—a good sign according to my pie man. We stand and gaze down at the thing in a moment of awe. My pie is done. My pie.

Suddenly, I long for an inviting windowsill on which to let it cool. I long to shoo away mischievous neighborhood youths with my apron: "Now you boys get away from there. That pie's not for you." I long to flaunt this pie before my friend who made the dare. I long for a church supper, a bake sale, a family dinner, so someone could ask what I brought and I could smugly say, "pie."

But there are none of these opportunities. There are only the two of us, and the two of us will sit down in the blue twilight of this coming summer evening, as couples have sat down to countless blue twilit Maine evenings for generations, and top off supper with blueberry pie.

And the pie will be fine.

Elizabeth Peavey, 2000

An old Maine recipe is just as much of an heirloom as a lovely antique.

Marjorie Standish, 1969